john coltrane's
giant steps

remixed by
chris raschka

A RICHARD JACKSON BOOK · Atheneum Books for Young Readers · NEW YORK   LONDON   TORONTO   SYDNEY   SINGAPORE

Atheneum Books for Young Readers
An imprint of Simon & Schuster Children's
Publishing Division
1230 Avenue of the Americas
New York, New York 10020

Book design by Ann Bobco
The text of this book is set in Broadband ICG.
The illustrations are rendered in watercolor and ink.

Manufactured in China   1210 SCP
10 9 8 7 6

Library of Congress Cataloging-in-Publication Data
Raschka, Christopher.
John Coltrane's Giant steps / Chris Raschka.—1st ed.
p.   cm.
"A Richard Jackson book."
Summary: John Coltrane's musical composition is
performed by a box, a snowflake, some raindrops, and
a kitten.
ISBN 978-0-689-84598-7
[1. Jazz—Fiction.]
PZ7.R1814 Gi 2002
[E]—dc21   2001033755

To Robert

Good evening. And thank you for coming to our book.
We have something very special for you tonight.

It's John Coltrane's marvelous and tricky composition, "Giant Steps," performed for you by a box, a snowflake, some raindrops, and a kitten.

Why not stay and see it?

While our performers are limbering up, let me say a few words about the composer. John Coltrane played soprano saxophone (little) and tenor saxophone (big)

and wrote music which, in his hands, became swirling, leaping, tumbling "sheets of sound." That's what he called it. But why tell you when we can show you?

Ready, my friends?

All right. Raindrops, start us off with a nice tempo.

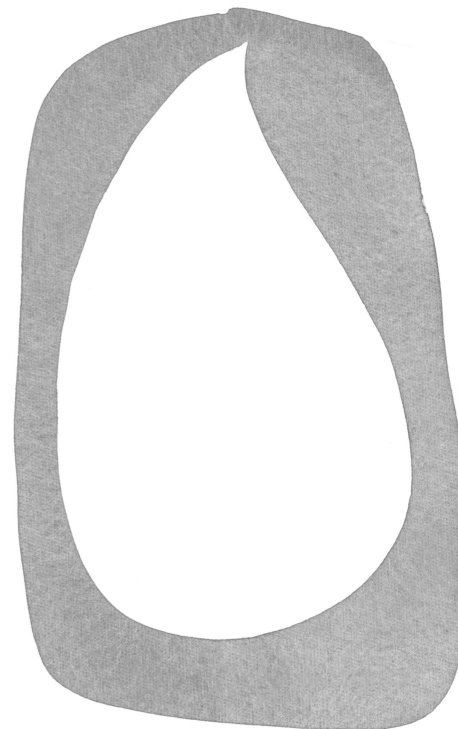

8

Make it not too fast and not too slow.

Lovely.

And here comes our box, our base,

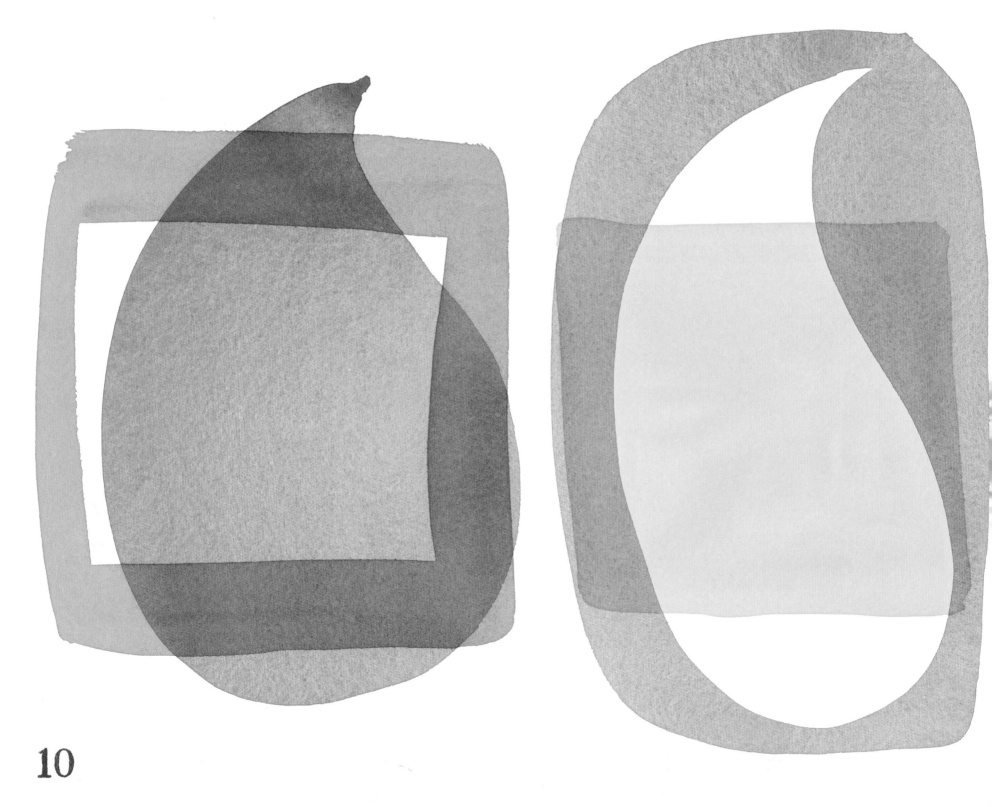

the sound foundation,

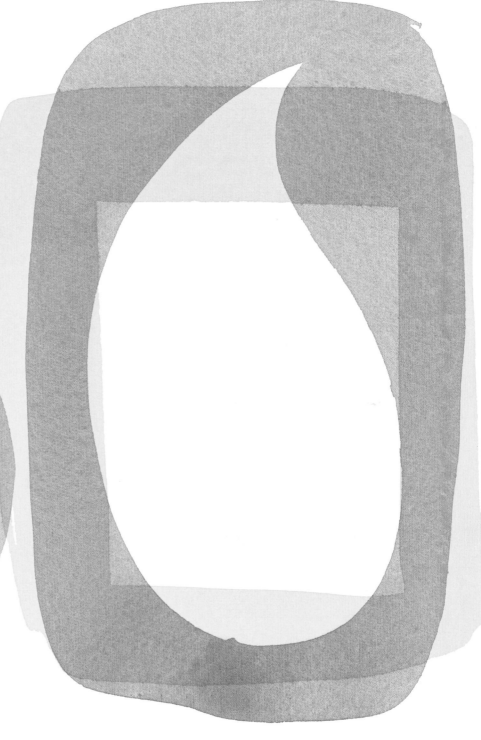

the bottom. It's something to build on.

Hello, snowflake. Our snowflake is taking the piano part tonight,

showing us the harmony, the beautiful frame.

Niceness.

Here's our kitten. She's the melody on top of everything.

Watch her take some giant steps across the page.

Meow!

Uh-huh. That's it.

BIG, BIG STEPS!

Steady.

Steady!   1   2   3   4   !

Hey.   Whoa!   Careful!   19

stop!

People, people! What happened?
Okay, okay, let's take a look at some trouble spots.

First of all,
raindrops,
you were
rushing on page 19.
Your drops
were much too
close together.
Keep in mind,
when you hear
John Coltrane playing,
no matter how fast he's going,
he always sounds relaxed.
It's as if he made time
bigger.

Now box,
box, my friend.
Much too heavy
on page 18.
I know you're our
foundation and
you've got to be strong.
But can you be strong
yet light?
Hmmmmm?
Try.

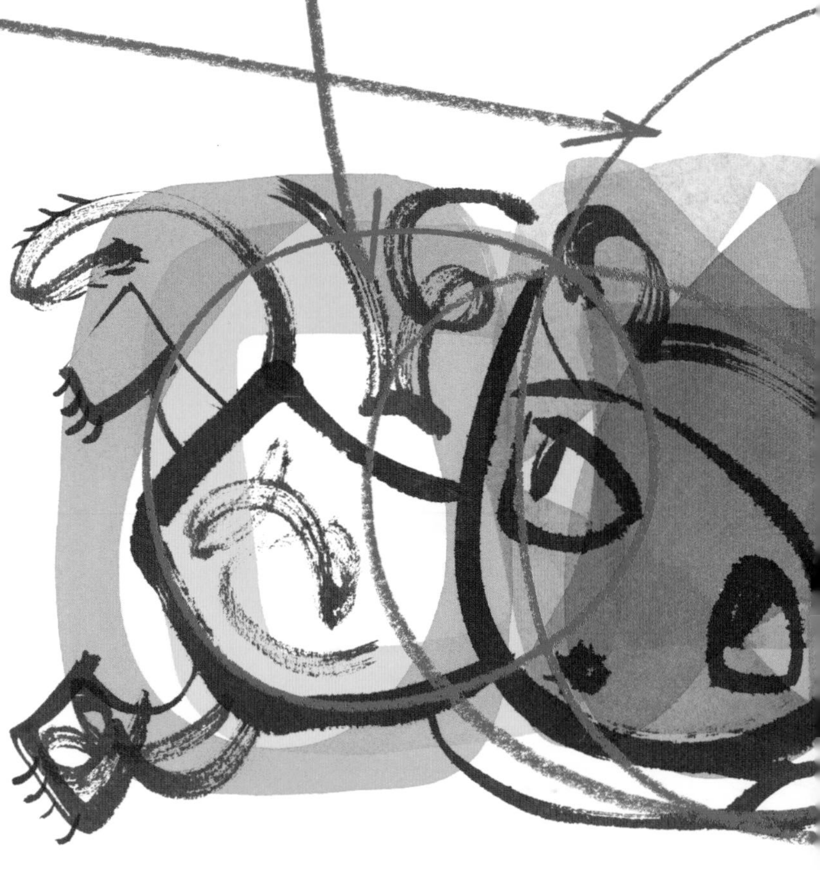

Snowflake. I like what you're doing,
I do. However, your color
is making me a little crazy.
What I want to see is rich color
but not muddy color.
Remember: Coltrane's music
is dense but transparent.
Okay?

Finally, kitten.
Lovely big steps.
Only thing:
On page 18,
you look a little blurry to me.
Is there any way
you can be more clear?
When John Coltrane
played his saxophone,
he blew a fountain of notes,
a shower of notes,
but those notes made lines
that were dynamic
and strong and vivid.
I know you're just a kitten
drawn on a page,
but see if you can be
more like
Mr. *Trane.*

All right, everyone?

Let's take it from page 14. Raindrop, box, snowflake, kitten.

Go.

27

Sheets of color.

Sheets of sound.

Bravo.

Bravo,

everyone.